guide to
Meditation

BROCKHAMPTON PRESS
LONDON

© 1996 Geddes & Grosset Ltd, David Dale House,
New Lanark ML11 9DJ

This edition published 1996 by Brockhampton Press, a member
of Hodder Headline PLC Group

ISBN 1 86019 298 X

Printed and bound in the UK

Contents

1

Introduction

'Select a clean spot, neither too high nor too low, and seat yourself firmly on a cloth, a deerskin, or kusha grass. Then, once seated, strive to still your thoughts. Make your mind one-pointed in meditation and your heart will be purified . . .'

These words come from the *Bhagavad Gita,* the best known and most influential of the Hindu scriptures. The book devotes an entire section to the practice of meditation, which is central to the Hindu way of life. It is also an integral part of the other great oriental religions, Buddhism and its close cousin Zen.

But while meditation is married in the minds of many to the East, it also has its place in Sufism, Christianity and Judaism. (That said, meditation does not require adherence to any of the faiths and religions that advocate it.)

Many people view meditation as peaceful but ineffectual self-centredness; in the words of one cynic, 'a form of self-indulgent passive introversion'. They are wrong—the benefits to be gained from meditation in any of its various forms are many. Those who meditate regularly believe that it leads to a significant lowering of tension and negative emotions while at the same time increasing efficiency at work and deepening the sense of inner calm.

This feeling of wellbeing brings physical benefits, for regular meditation eliminates or reduces stress, and who in the helter-skelter days of the late twentieth century is not stressed at some time or other? In reducing stress, meditation can ease migraine and tension headaches, reduce blood pressure, benefit the heart and reduce the agony of menstrual cramps.

What is meditation?

In its simplest form, meditation is nothing more than allowing the mind to be lulled by a simple repetitive sensation—waves lapping on the beach, the tinkling of a fountain, repeating a word or sound over and over again, even something as mundane as the sound of machinery Any of these, and countless others, can be used as something onto which the mind focuses so strongly that problems and anxieties are crowded out. In its more refined, mystical guise, it is a means to total self-fulfilment, being completely at one with the universe.

Meditation is neither a time-consuming process (twenty minutes a day are all that is needed), nor is it, as many suspect, a form of self-hypnosis. Practised properly, it is a life-enhancing voyage during which preconceived opinions and ideas fade, the senses and the intellect are refined, and the ability to concentrate is increased.

Its benefits quickly become apparent, and those who practise it often say that the day they first took to meditation on a regular basis was a watershed in their lives.

Meditation and contemplation

Confusion sometimes arises when the words 'meditation' and 'contemplation' are used interchangeably. A working distinction between the two is that meditation can be considered a preparatory step and contributory to the achievement of contemplation.

Meditation involves concentration, narrowing the focus of attention to a single theme, catechism or doctrine while remaining cognitive and intellectual. Contemplation is a direct intuitive seeing, using spiritual facilities that are beyond discursive thought. In the words of Richard of Saint-Victor, a twelfth-century theologian, 'Meditation investigates, contemplation wonders.'

The need for a teacher

No one in their right mind would sit down at a piano and expect to play a Chopin nocturne if they had never played before. So why should someone who is about to meditate for the first time expect to sit down and expect to lose themselves in meditation right away? Like all things worth doing, the best way to learn meditation is to study with someone who has already mastered it. If we are to compare the mind with a piano in order to create beautiful music, we need to study with an expert who is familiar with the instrument and who can help us gain mastery over it.

A good teacher must be qualified, compassionate, expert, patient, sincere and sympathetic, someone in whom the pupil may have complete confidence—but where to find such a paragon? Some novices are lucky and find the right 'guru' straightaway. Others may take months, even years before they meet the one that is right for them. Those who fall into the latter category should not be disheartened: they should carry on practising basic meditation techniques, trying different teachers and following their own judgement until, eventually, they find someone who can help them to get the most out of meditation.

Some people, unable to find a suitable teacher, turn to one or other of the many audio tapes on the market aimed at the increasing numbers of people who are turning to meditation either for health or spiritual reasons. Before committing yourself to the expense of buying one, inquire at your local library to find out if it has an audio section. If there is such a tape on its shelves, borrow it for a few days to find out if it helps you.

Keeping a level head

Where you meditate and when you meditate is up to you, but a word of advice—don't be tempted to adopt a holier-than-thou attitude among friends and colleagues. They may, after some weeks or months, realize that you appear to be calmer and more relaxed and that you have subtly changed in some way or other that they cannot put their finger on. They may ask you what has brought about the change. Then by all means tell them that you have taken up meditating but broadcasting your experiences can defeat the object of the exercise!

Caveat!

Meditation is not suitable for everyone. Anyone who is suffering from clinical depression or any mild form of mental illness should first consult their doctor.

It should never be used as a substitute for medical treatment, and anyone on any form of medication, should likewise consult their doctor.

Meditation creates an altered state of consciousness. Newcomers have no way of knowing how they will respond to it, so it is best to limit the first few sessions to ten minutes at most.

Finally, meditation should not be seen as a panacea. It should be seen as a means to an end, not as the end in itself.

Crossing the bridge

In his book *Complete Meditation*, American guru Steve Kravette wrote, 'By practising meditation and being completely who you are, you will become more than you are now. You will be able to cross the next evolutionary bridge and begin to develop the full potential of your creaturehood.'

Meditation is a journey, enjoy it.

2

Meditation in the World's Religions

Buddhism

Meditation lies at the very centre of Buddhism, the term used in the West to describe the teachings of an Indian prince, Guatama Siddhartha, who lived from c.563 BC to 483 BC. Siddhartha's wealthy father did everything he could to protect his son from the evils of the world, and it was not until the young man was in his late twenties that he saw a beggar, a sick man, a decrepit old man and a corpse for the first time and realized just how privileged he was. When he asked a wandering monk about sickness and suffering, the mendicant told him that misery and pain were part and parcel of everyday life. Inspired by the monk's example, Siddhartha left his wife and family and turned his back on wealth and self-indulgence.

At first he looked to Hinduism for answers to the problems of suffering, but finding no answers in the faith of his ancestors, he began to conduct his own search for the truth and meaning of life.

Six years later, sitting deep in thought in the shade of a bo tree on the banks of the Neranjari River he achieved enlightenment, and seeing it as his duty to help others along the path he had trodden for so long, he began to preach his message.

At the heart of Buddhism lie the Four Noble Truths:
—all life is suffering
—suffering is caused by selfish desires
—putting an end to these desires stops suffering
—the way to end suffering is to follow the Eightfold Path.

This path demands that those who seek enlightenment must trust in the Four Noble Truths until they can see them for themselves. They must have the right values, the right speech,

9

conduct themselves in the right manner and have the right means of livelihood. They must endeavour in the right way, have right control of their minds and have the right kind of meditation.

One of the major disciplines of the Buddhist meditator is to attain 'unification of the mind' by eliminating all distractions. As the practitioner learns to meditate for long periods, agitation, scepticism and doubt disappear and are replaced by a feeling of bliss. The meditator becomes absorbed in thought (a process known as *jhana*) and moves deeper and deeper until he or she finally acquires an awareness of infinite space.

Many Buddhists regard the pursuit of various *jhana* levels as secondary to the 'Path of Mindfulness', which in the end leads to *nirvana*. The meditator learns to break out of stereotyped thought and comes to perceive every moment of everyday reality as if it were a new event. The ego shrinks in importance; the universe is seen to be in a state of total and ever-changing flux. This realization leads to a sense of detachment from the world of experience, an abandonment of all desires, the abolition of self-interest and, ultimately, the ego itself.

Meditation can take place anywhere, for Buddhism is essentially a religion for the individual. Meditation is not a communal act. Even within organized Buddhist communities, the way one meditates is a matter for the individual and not for the community. There is no prescribed pattern of worship for Buddhists. They may, if they so wish, visit pagodas, temples and shrines and focus on something there while meditating. But it is equally proper for them to meditate in their own homes, sitting in whichever position they choose (usually cross-legged) on the floor.

Some Buddhist families may have a statue of the Buddha in a specially built shrine in their homes; some burn incense and use prayer beads to help them concentrate the mind; some use mantras and mandalas, while others simply adopt their usual meditative position and quickly lose themselves in meditation.

It is estimated that more than 300 million people around the world practise Buddhism, and it is an interesting comment on late twentieth-century life that more and more young people in the West are treading the same path and that Buddhism is one of the fastest-growing religions in the Western world.

Zen Buddhism

According to legend, in AD 520 the Indian thinker Bodhidharma (the first patriarch of Zen Buddhism) journeyed from India to China, where he presented himself at the court of the Emperor Wu, a devout Buddhist. When the emperor asked Bodhidharma what merit he, the emperor, had gained on the Path to Enlightenment by building temples and assiduously copying holy writings, the Indian incurred his wrath by telling him that there was no merit in such deeds as they showed worldly attachment. True merit was only to be found in acts of absolute wisdom, beyond the realm of rational thought. Truth, said Bodhidharma, is emptiness, and holiness for holiness' sake has nothing to recommend it.

Wu was so furious with Bodhidharma's doctrine that the Indian left court and spent several years in a monastery contemplating a wall. He later communicated his thoughts and teachings—the *Visuddhimagga,* or Path to Purification, which describes the meditative approach from the Buddhist point of view—to Hui-k'o who thus became the second patriarch of Zen Buddhism.

Meditation has always been a keystone of Buddhism. Zen teaches that it is everything. Its followers do not believe in rituals or reading the Buddha's sermons (*sutras*). In Zen, meditation is more total and more intense than in any other Buddhist sect. The Buddhist who follows the Zen path must strive to avoid all conscious thought except the point on which he or she is meditating (*see* Zen Meditation page 56).

11

There is a famous story of a man who went to a Zen master and asked to be taught Zen. The master said nothing but poured the seeker a cup of tea, using a cup that was already full, and kept pouring until the pot was empty. Then he spoke. 'You are like this cup,' he said. 'You are full. How can I pour Zen into you? Empty yourself and come back.'

Christianity

Modern Christianity stresses the importance of doing good deeds, loving one's neighbour and avoiding sin; the mystical side of the religion has largely been swept aside. But Christianity is essentially a mystical religion, for the true Christian seeks to be united with God through following the way of Christ, who said, 'I am the way, the truth and the light. No one comes to the Father except through me.'

Meditation should play an important part in Christian worship, and it is interesting to note in this respect the volume of music that has been composed down the centuries to encourage meditation. Traditional Christian teaching advocates meditation as a means of getting closer to God. St Teresa of Avila, for example, recommended the *via positiva*—concentrating the mind on God's love and absolute goodness in order to acquire some sense of His magnitude.

It is through such contemplation that the Christian meditator strives to overcome the limitations of conscious thought and achieve a state of ecstasy in the perfect union with God in love and adoration.

Meditation is still widely practised in monasteries, convents and other religious communities, and more and more Christians are spending time 'in retreat', sometimes for a day or two, sometimes for longer, in quiet contemplation.

Christian meditation usually concentrates on the life of Jesus, Mary and the saints, and the most common aid to meditation is probably the Crucifix, although some Christians find that their concentration is heightened if they repeat the name of Jesus or Mary or recite short prayers while they meditate (*see* Mantras page 36).

Hinduism

It is probably with yoga that most Westerners associate meditation. A few years ago the mention of the word would conjure up images of scraggy men, dressed in loincloths, sitting in a meditative trance, and stories of yogis who had been in such a state for so long that birds had nested on their heads were widely circulated to general amusement. Westerners who 'did yoga' were regarded at best as cranks, but today, with more and more people in the West taking it up and with an awakening interest in oriental religion generally, if someone confesses to trying yoga, the reaction is generally one of interest and an expressed desire to know more.

The watershed for the increased interest in yoga meditation probably came in the 1960s with the huge publicity given to the pop groups who travelled to India and returned extolling the virtues of transcendental meditation. But what was new to the West has been practised for thousands of years in the subcontinent.

There is no formal creed in Hinduism, rather a number of religious concepts have developed and have been elaborated since it was founded, probably about 3000 years ago. These ideas were centred on the aim of every Hindu, which is to attain ultimate freedom, or *moksha,* to be free of the endless cycle of rebirths and to be at one with Brahman—the one ultimate reality. Humans learn through yoga (the word derives from the Sanskrit *yuj,* meaning 'to bind together') to achieve this union.

Yoga, the means of gaining liberation from the senses, is one of the four main concepts that underlie Hindu spiritual philosophy. The others are *karma,* the law of causality that links mankind to the universe, *maya,* the illusion of the

13

manifest world, and *nirvana,* the absolute reality that lies beyond illusion. (*See* page 58)

Yoga encourages the practitioner to see things as they are rather than as they seem. All bodily and mental tensions must cease to be if this is to be so, and, accordingly, one of the basic yoga techniques is meditation as this turns consciousness towards inner calm and finally transcendence.

Judaism

'When a man strips away the material aspect which envelops him, he will depict in his mind only the divine energy, so that its light will be of infinite greatness.' The words of Rabbi Dov Baer underline the importance of meditation in Jewish mysticism, which has its roots in the Kaballa, the movement that combines a complex system of philosophy with specific techniques for increasing spiritual awareness.

Kaballistic teaching holds that everything in the universe is derived from one source and that the purpose of our existence is to recognize our identity with God and all of creation through meditation and other spiritual practices.

Kaballistic Jews most often practise visual meditation (*see* page 43), focusing their thoughts on the Tree of Life or the characters of the Jewish alphabet, each of which is said to contain an aspect of the creative energy. Jews who follow the meditative path claim that they are open to a state of awareness that transcends their normal level of consciousness. They hold that their physical health also benefits. This is in line with the teaching of early Jewish mystics, who recognized the relationship between a person's state of mind and his or her physical wellbeing.

Sufism

Some say that Sufism (the word comes from 'sufi' and was originally applied to someone who wore *suf,* or undyed wool) developed from Islam. Others believe that it developed as a reaction against it. Whatever its origins, most Sufis are Muslim, although the latter is not a prerequisite of the former, and non-Islamic Sufi groups are found in many parts of the world.

Sufis base their beliefs on certain passages of the Koran, and some early Christian ideas. Their aim is to transcend everyday thought processes and to achieve a mystical union of the physical, the spiritual and the mental. The Sufist way of life involves fasting, storytelling, dancing and meditation.

There are many different types of meditation. Perhaps the strangest is one practised by a particular group of Sufists—the whirling dervishes who achieve a state of meditative ecstasy by spinning round and round at an ever-increasing rate, hoping to empty the mind of everything apart from communicating with God. Most forms of meditation can be easily practised at home. This one should not.

3

Getting Down to it

Having decided that meditation is something you would like to try, maybe for relaxation, maybe from more mystical motives, what is the next move? Before going on to look at meditation techniques, there are some basics that should first be considered.

Posture
It is essential to adopt the correct position, not necessarily a sitting one, when meditating. Many practitioners of the art consider that the centuries-old seven-point posture is the best for helping to achieve a calm, clear state of mind and has yet to be bettered.

Others recommend the Siddhasana, while many beginners opt for a simple cross-legged position (the easy posture), sitting in a chair (Egyptian posture) or kneeling with the buttocks on the ankles (Japanese posture).

Easy posture
Basically, this involves sitting cross-legged with both feet on the floor. The back should be straight but not tense and the stomach muscles relaxed. With the muscles of the lower back bearing the weight of the body and with the head, neck and trunk in line, the centre of gravity passes from the base of the spine right through the top of the head. The hands can either be resting lightly on the knees or held in the lap, either one on top of the other or clasped lightly.

Siddhasana
Sitting on the floor with the back straight, stretch the legs out in front of you. Bend the left knee and, grasping the left foot with both hands, draw it towards the body until the heel is resting against the part of the lower body that lies between the anus

and genitalia. Now draw the right foot towards the body until the heel is on the pubic bone. Tuck the toes of the right foot between the calf and the thigh of the left leg. Rest the hands, palms upwards on the knees. Siddhasana is sometimes called the perfect posture.

Seven-point posture

1. If possible, try to sit with the legs crossed in the lotus position, or *varja*, with each foot placed sole upwards on the thigh of the opposite leg. To get into the lotus position loosen up with the exercises on pages 18-19 and then sit on the floor, legs stretched out in front of you. Now bend the right knee and, grasping the right foot with both hands, place it on top of the left thigh, heel pressing into the abdomen. Repeat the process with the left foot. The soles should be turned up, with both knees on the ground.

   If you cannot get into the full lotus position, try the half-lotus. Do the same seven exercises before stretching the legs out in front of you. Bend the left knee and put the left foot beneath the right thigh, as close to the buttock as you can get it. Now bend the right knee and put the right foot, sole up, on top of the left thigh. Keep both knees on the ground and the back straight. When you find that you can maintain this position comfortably throughout the session over a period of four or five weeks, you will be able to start trying the full lotus.

   Sitting on a hard cushion will encourage you to keep the back straight and help you to sit for longer without getting irritating pins and needles in the legs and feet.

2. The hands should be held loosely on the lap about a centimetre below the navel, right hand on top of left, palms upwards, fingers aligned. Both hands should be slightly cupped so that the tips of the thumbs meet to form a triangle. The shoulders and arms should be relaxed. Never be tempted to press the arms against the body—they should be held a few centimetres away to allow the air to circulate which helps prevent feelings of drowsiness.

3. The back must be straight but relaxed. Try to imagine the spinal

17

vertebrae as a pile of two-pence pieces, delicately balanced one on top of the other that will crash to the ground if it is disturbed. A straight back encourages the energy to flow freely, and you will be able to meditate for longer and longer periods.

4. Many newcomers to meditation find it easier to concentrate with the eyes fully closed. This is not wrong, but it is better to gaze downwards through slightly open eyes. Closed eyes encourage sleepiness and dreamlike images that mar meditation.

5. The jaw and mouth should both be relaxed, the teeth slightly apart, the lips lightly together.

6. Keep the tongue touching the palate just behind the upper teeth to reduce the flow of saliva and thus the need to swallow.

7. Bend the neck forward so that your gaze is directed to the floor in front of you. Don't drop it too low: this encourages sleepiness.

The seven point position keeps the body and mind comfortable and free of tension. Beginners should not expect to be able to adopt it right away; it takes time to master.

Seven simple exercises

Before trying to assume the lotus position, try these floor exercises to loosen the joints affected. Try to maintain a straight back and fixed head position throughout each exercise.

1. Stretch the legs straight out in front of you. Bend your right knee so that you can grasp the right ankle with both hands and put it on the left leg just above the knee so that the right foot is extending beyond the left leg. Keeping a firm grip on the ankle with the right hand, use the left hand to rotate the foot ten times in one direction and ten times in the other. Repeat the exercise with the left ankle and foot on the right leg.

2. Sitting in the same position as for the first exercise, put the right knee on the left leg as before and with both hands grasping the right ankle, lift it above the leg and shake the foot for twenty seconds. Repeat with the other leg.

3. Place the right foot on the left leg as before. Holding the foot in the left hand and wrapping the right hand around the leg at the ankle, lift the right leg as high as you can and make a large

circle with the foot, drawing it close to the body at the top of the circle and pushing it away at the bottom. Repeat ten times before doing the same with the other leg.

4. With the palms of the hands flat on the floor behind and beyond the buttocks, bend the right knee and place the right foot as high up the left thigh as you can comfortably get it with the right knee as close to the ground as possible. Hold this position for a minute and then repeat with the other leg.

5. Supporting the body with the left hand flat on the floor in the same position as for the last exercise, put the right foot as high up the left thigh as possible, place the right hand on the right knee and gently bounce for a count of ten. Repeat with the left leg.

6. Stretch the legs out in front of you and then slowly bend the knees outwards and draw the soles of the feet together. With the soles touching each other, bring the heels as close to the groin as possible and then, holding the toes with both hands, bounce the knees ten times, keeping them as close to the floor as possible. Hold for a count of ten.

7. Do the same as for the last exercise, but when the heels are as close to the groin as you can get them, put the hands on the knees and press them as far down to the floor as you can. Again, hold for a count of ten.

The sitting position

Older people, or those with back problems who are unable to sit on the floor, can sit on a chair or on a low bench and lose themselves in meditation just as effectively as the more supple.

The ideal chair is one specially designed to encourage good posture: the chair is backless and has a slanted seat and knee rest. A straight-backed chair can also be used, in which case, sit on the front part of the seat with the feet flat on the floor and the legs slightly apart, the lower legs perpendicular to the floor.

It is inadvisable to meditate while sitting in an armchair or on the edge of a bed as the upholstery encourages you to slouch and become drowsy.

Kneeling

Some people find this a convenient and comfortable position for meditation as it is easy to keep the spine straight. Simply kneel on the floor, keeping the knees together. Part the heels and bring the toes together so that you are sitting, straight-backed, on the insides of the feet with the hands on the knees.

Lying flat

This position is called *shavasanaor,* the corpse position. Lie flat on the floor on a carpet, blanket or hard mattress. Part the legs a little and let the feet flop to the side. The arms should be slightly away from the body, hands on the floor, palms up.

Some teachers encourage their pupils to take up this position and relax for a short time before assuming one of the other positions for the meditation session. Relaxing like this prepares the mind for the meditation proper. When you are in the corpse position, starting with the toes and working upwards to the brow, flex each muscle and shake each joint and then relax it before moving on to the next. When you have flexed the face muscles, go back to the beginning and tell each muscle to relax.

At first, some people feel self-conscious lying on their back and saying aloud, 'Toes relax!', 'Feet relax!' and so on. Their self-consciousness soon evaporates when they realize that the method works. When you are completely relaxed lie still for a few minutes, simply concentrating on your breathing before starting the meditation proper or assuming one of the other positions.

Cupping the hands

Some teachers recommend that the hands be cupped if the pupil is in a posture where it is appropriate to do so. Right-handed people who decide to do this should cup the left hand over the right and, similarly, left-handed pupils should cup the right hand over the left, the point being to immobilize the dominant hand.

4

The Meditation Session

Once you are sitting comfortably in the seven-point posture, *Siddhasana,* or whichever of the other recommended positions suits you best, spend a minute or two settling your body and mind, deciding which meditation you will do and how long you will meditate.

Some meditators prostrate themselves three times before settling down to meditate, believing that this counteracts pride, which is a barrier to effective meditation.

Now run through your thoughts. Set your goals. Why are you about to meditate? What do you hope to achieve by it? The more motivated you are and the clearer your goal, the more successful the meditation is likely to be.

Many people take up meditation simply to relax, but the more experienced they become the more far-reaching are their aims, and they feel themselves drawn to the more mystical side of meditation—the search for an understanding of the nature of reality.The deeper they search, the calmer, happier and more satisfied they become. Some go too far! They assume a smug, self-satisfied attitude that is not just off-putting to others but defeats the whole object of the exercise.

Which technique?
There are many different methods of meditation. Some have been handed down from generation to generation for thousands of years and remain in their pure form. Others have been adapted to suit current circumstances. Deciding which of them is right for you can be quite bewildering, but bear in mind that the techniques are not ends in themselves: they are the motorway on which the journey to meditation moves.

The best technique for you is the one with which you feel most comfortable.

Experiment

Start perhaps with breath-awareness techniques, which are the simplest. Many people go no further. Others experiment with different techniques until they find another method they prefer or they come back to breath awareness. Despite the extravagant claims made by the followers of their own particular favourite, there is no technique that is better than any of the others.

Try not to decide on a method after just one session. Give it a trial run over a week or two, jotting down the frame of mind you were in before you went into meditation and how you felt when you came out of it. At the end of the trial period, try and see if that particular method has improved the quality of your life. If it has, and you feel comfortable with it, stick to it, for by using a method that suits you and making it part of your life you will make much faster progress than if you dabble in one and then move on to another just for experiment's sake.

Proper breathing

This is vital to proper meditation. Generally, you should breathe in at your normal rate through the nose. Don't be tempted to force yourself to breathe more deeply or more slowly than usual. You will probably find that the deeper you meditate, the slower and more deeply you will breathe.

A technique called bellows breathing, or *bhastrika pranayama,* is recommended by experienced meditators to quieten the mind before meditation proper begins. The practice involves breathing in and out rapidly by forcing the abdominal muscles to expand and contract rapidly. It takes a great deal of practice to breathe properly in this way, and even those who have mastered the technique should never try it until at least three hours after eating, and they should eat nothing for at least half an hour afterwards.

It should be noted that breathing in this way can produce dizziness and nausea and should never be practised by pregnant women, anyone with hyper- or hypo-tension or with heart or lung problems. It is best learned from a teacher than from the pages of a book such as this.

The time . . .

There are no set rules as to how often you should meditate—some people meditate every day, others find just once a week suits them. It doesn't matter, as long as you meditate regularly, but remember that if you let too long a period elapse between sessions you will be as out of shape, meditatively speaking, as ballet dancers would be if they didn't go to a class regularly. There will certainly be days when you are due to meditate when it is the last thing you want to do, but try anyway, even if only for a few minutes. It is best not to meditate for at least two hours after eating a meal.

. . . and the place

If you have a large house, reserve a room specially for meditation, but if space is a problem, set aside a corner of a suitable room. Put a mat on the floor close to a table or bench for books you may need for your meditation, or for the picture or image on which you are going to focus your thoughts.

Make sure the area is clean, quiet and as pleasing as you can make it so that it is somewhere you will look forward to being in. Make sure, too, that you tell your family you don't want to be disturbed while you are meditating.

Some people burn candles and incense sticks. If you think they will help you to meditate or make the room more conducive to meditation by all means follow their example. Remember that to meditate effectively you must be as relaxed as possible.

The meditation object

This is something on which the attention can focus and on

which it may rest, ideally for the full session, although in practice this rarely happens as even experienced meditators may find their attention wandering at some time or other (*see* below), but the meditation object is always there to come back to.

The object may be something to look at—a flower, a candle, a religious icon or a *mandala* or *yantra,* symbols specially designed for meditation. It may be something you can listen to—a cassette recording the sound of the sea or a running river or birdsong, for example. It can be as everyday as the ticking of the clock or as esoteric as the tinkling of temple bells.

Many meditators use a *mantra,* a word or phrase repeated again and again either out loud or mentally.

The meditation object can even be your own breath.

These are all discussed in more detail on pages in chapters 7 and 8..

Problems

Even the most practised meditators may experience difficulties, so beginners should not be put off if they find it hard to get into a meditative state of mind or to maintain concentration.

One of the most common problems is mental excitement. The mind becomes restless and the attention is continually distracted. Sometimes we are unable to banish nagging problems from our thoughts—for example, job security, paying household bills, health worries. If we are in a particularly good frame of mind, we may unintentionally recall things that have made us smile—a new friendship, an enjoyable conversation, even a television programme we have enjoyed.

In our everyday lives we let our minds jump from thought to thought, from worry to worry, so mental wandering is a deeply ingrained habit and, like any habit, is difficult to give up. One popular way of overcoming it is to concentrate on breathing, which has a very calming effect on one's state of mind.

Be patient. It takes time and constant practice to learn how to slow down and control the mind. Don't give up. Even an experienced meditator such as St Teresa of Avila experienced difficulties. When she overheard a novice at her convent remark that it must be wonderful to 'be like Sister Teresa' and not be bothered by distractions during her prayers and meditations, she surprised the girl by saying, 'What do you think I am, a saint?'

Another common problem is drowsiness. When we are in a completely relaxed frame of mind, it is all too easy to drop off. If you start to feel sleepy while meditating, make sure that you are sitting up straight and your head is not bent too far forward. If youare meditating with your eyes closed, open them and meditate with the gaze directed at the floor just in front of you. If you are meditating in a centrally heated room, turn down the heating or open a window to freshen the air. Increasing the amount of light in the room can also help you to stay awake.

Physical tension

Any physical discomfort makes effective meditation difficult. Often such discomfort is a physical manifestation of mental turmoil—it could be an unresolved problem or worry, or something that has made you angry. So if your meditation is disrupted by physical discomfort for no obvious reason, then try to recognize any such problems and settle it in meditation.

One way of getting rid of physical tension is to focus your attention for a moment on each part of the body in turn, starting with the head and working downwards, making a conscious effort to make it relax. You can do this at the start of the session or during it if need be.

Deep, slow breathing can also help. Concentrate as hard as you can, and as you breathe out, try to imagine the pain or tension evaporating.

Long-term benefits

Try not to expect too much too quickly. Don't think that because you have been meditating every day for a week or two and feel absolutely no benefit, meditation is not working for you. It can take months, sometimes years, for positive changes to manifest themselves, and even when they do, they can happen over such an extended period you may not be aware of the difference regular meditation is making to you. Others, however, will certainly realize that something about you has changed for the better.

Breaking the spell

Avoid coming out of meditation too quickly, for if you do, most of the benefits you have achieved will be lost. Once you have finished meditating remain in your meditative position for a minute or two and then slowly stretch, catlike, quietly reflecting on how good you now feel—calmer and better equipped to cope with everyday living. Instead of acting impulsively or emotionally, you will be more thoughtful and better equipped to deal with lif's problems.

5

Breathing Meditations

Awareness of breath

Correct abdominal breathing lies at the heart of all kinds of meditation. In 'awareness of breath' meditation, breathing itself is the object of the meditation. Such meditation is held in the highest regard among Buddhists, Hindus and Taoists, all of whom believe in it not just as a means of inducing peace of mind but also of encouraging physical and mental health.

Breathing awareness can also be used as a prelude to another form of meditation. If this is to be the case, five minutes or so will calm the nerves and focus and still the mind, putting it in a receptive mood for the session proper.

Awareness of breath meditation techniques are ideal for the novice meditator because they are entirely natural and most people feel quite comfortable with them. The techniques simply involve being aware of the breath as it enters and leaves the body.

Sit motionless in any of the postures you find comfortable, remembering to keep the back, head and neck in perfect balance, and begin to think about your breathing, becoming aware of each intake of breath, the pause, the expulsion of stale air from the lungs, the pause, the next breath. Your attention will wander. Don't be put off; bring it back to the object of your meditation and start again on the next inhalation.

It is not unusual for the pattern of breathing to change during meditation. At first, when you may be feeling a little self-conscious, you may find that you are holding each breath for longer than usual, but as the meditation proceeds you should find that breathing becomes smoother and deeper, or it may become shallow and slow. Don't be concerned by this. As you concentrate on your breathing and lose yourself in the meditation, the body establishes a rate of breathing that is right for that particular time.

There are several methods for encouraging attention to focus on the breath. None of them is better than any of the others. Try them all, and if you are happier with one over the rest, stick with it. Naturally they all require you to adopt a suitable posture and choose an appropriate place. One newcomer to breath awareness meditation decided to try it in a stuffy underground train. He closed his eyes, put his thoughts in order, began to breathe in and out as he had learned . . . and was woken by the guard when the train reached the terminus many stops past his own.

The simplest methods

Take up a comfortable posture. You may shut your eyes to aid concentration, but it is better to keep them half open. Breathe as naturally as you can, counting either each inhalation or exhalation up to ten, and repeat this for twenty minutes. Counting is an aid to concentration and helps to prevent the mind from wandering.

Some people find it helps if they focus their attention on the tip of the nose or the inside of the nostrils as the breath enters and leaves the body. Others use the movement of the abdomen as the focus of their attention.

Mindfulness of breathing meditation

'A monk having gone to the forest, to the foot of a tree, or to an empty place, sits down cross-legged, keeps his body erect and his mindfulness alert. Just mindful he breathes in and mindful he breathes out.'

Thus did the Suddha advocate to his followers mindfulness of breathing meditation, also called 'following the breath'.

According to this widely practised method of meditation, the abdomen or nose is the focus of attention, which is a development of basic awareness of breath meditation which many people find unsatisfying after a month or two.

There is no counting in mindfulness of breath meditation, rather it is the flow of breath in and out on which the mind is concentrated. To practise it, sit comfortably in any of the prescribed positions with the eyes closed and breathe in and out quite naturally, focusing the attention either on the abdomen or the nose.

If it's the abdomen, become aware of the pause in breathing at the limit of each sea-swell-like rise and fall of the abdomen. If it's the nose, concentrate on the nostrils where the flow of inhaled and exhaled air can be felt.

You are certain to find at first that your attention wanders even if you have been successfully practising counting the breath meditation for some time. When you realize that your attention has meandered, simply return it to the abdomen or nose and continue the meditation.

As you give in to the seductive rhythm of your abdomen as it rises and falls or your sensation of the inflow or outflow of air in the nostrils, your breathing will become smoother and much quieter as the meditation deepens.

Try to avoid controlling your breathing in any way. This can be difficult. Watching the breath without trying to interfere with it seems simple, but it takes some practice for the mind to become used to the fact that you are trying to surrender yourself completely to the spontaneous flow of the breath. Beginners usually find that their breathing becomes uneven, quickening and slowing for no apparent reason. They should not worry, for in time the breath settles to its own rhythm.

Many of those who practise following the breath meditation find it helps if they make themselves aware of the journey of each breath from the moment it enters the nostril to the moment it is expelled. Others picture an aura of energy and light just in front of the forehead. With each breath some of the power is taken into the body and the meditator focuses on its journey deep into the body.

Most of the faiths or religions that advocate breathing meditation have their own techniques. Zen Buddhists, for example, sometimes imagine that a ball of lead drops slowly through the body with each breath-making the stale deoxygenized air fall out.

Many have their own methods of dealing with the inevitable distractions. Some Buddhist teachers encourage their pupils to use the distractions themselves as the objects of meditation for a moment before they are dissolved and following the breath can be resumed.

6

Active Meditation

The Sufi circle

Most meditations are done on one's own or with a teacher.
Movement meditation as practised by some Sufis (best known
for their dramatic whirling dancing) is done by groups of five to
fifteen people and involves chanting as well.

Form a circle with your companions, standing with feet apart
some distance from each other but not so far that you have to
stretch your arms as you join hands. Now, very slowly lean
backwards raising your face to the ceiling (or sky if you are
doing this outdoors) and bring the hands up. When everyone is
comfortably looking as straight up as they can, say the words
'Ya Hai' loudly in unison. Now all the people in the group
brings their arms down and their heads and bodies forward,
until they are facing downwards. Now say in the sane ringing,
triumphant tone, 'Ya Huk', and return to the 'Ya Hai' position
and repeat again and again, establishing a speed and a rhythm
comfortable to everyone. Seen from above, the group looks like
a blossom opening and closing in perfect harmony.

The point of this meditation is total involvement of awareness of the movement and the accompanying sounds, and each
person must be conscious of the physical condition of each of
the others in the group. If someone finds that he or she is
having to push himself or herself to keep up with the group as
it establishes its rhythm, that person steps back and brings the
hands of the people on either side together so that the circle
remains intact. There must be complete freedom to do this. No
one should feel compelled to keep up: if so, the whole point of
the meditation is lost.

The aim is to go beyond fatigue to the point where exhaustion is forgotten and all are so lost in the movement and chanting that they become unaware of everything apart from the awareness of self and universe being in total harmony which is the point of all meditation.

Most groups start with ten- to fifteen-minute sessions to establish harmony and a rate at which everyone is comfortable, and when this is achieved, extend the sessions to half an hour.

Sensory awareness meditation

Movement is also a part of this sensory awareness meditation in which it is combined with breathing awareness.

Begin by lying on your back on a rug or mat. Your legs can be fully extended or drawn in towards the buttocks with the feet flat on the floor. When you are comfortable, close your eyes and concentrate for a few minutes on letting each part of the body in turn sink more deeply into the floor, starting with the feet and moving upwards through the calves, knees, thighs, pelvis, ribcage, chest, hands, lower arms, elbows, upper arms and neck to the head. Concentrate not just on the surfaces that are in contact with the floor but with the sides and top too.

Now, concentrating on each exhalation of breath, try to feel your whole body sink deeply into the floor.

After about fifteen minutes, lay the hands on the diaphragm, keeping the upper arms and elbows firmly on the floor. After the diaphragm has moved the hands up and down, up and down for a minute or two, they will feel as if they have been incorporated into the breathing process. Very slowly raise them a little from the body, concentrating all the time on your breathing, then return them to the diaphragm, allowing them once again to become part of the breathing process.

Repeat this for ten minutes or so, gradually increasing the distance the hands are moved away from the body each time until they eventually come to land on the floor. Slowly you will come to think that the whole cycle is happening by itself with absolutely no effort on your part, and you will find yourself at one with the world.

Tai Chi Ch'uan

Although it is not meditation in the accepted meaning of the word, the aim of Tai Chi (the 'Ch'uan' is usually dropped) is to combine motion, unity and dance so that those who practise its art surrender to the natural flow of the universe and become one with it—exactly the aim of more passive meditation.

Tai Chi is a means of exploring the processes of mind and body through creative movement and reflects the I Ching belief that nature is always in motion. It is said to have originated with the meditation of a Taoist monk, Chang San-feng, who one day saw a magpie trying to attack a snake. The reptile teased the bird by writhing and curling in a spiral motion, always remaining just out of the bird's reach. Similar movements are now an integral part of Tai Chi.

In Tai Chi, the image of water symbolizes the flow of energy. It represents the way the flow of energy yields to the form of its container. Earth is seen as a link between person and planet. The use of circular forms of expression shows unity and containment.

It is not possible to learn Tai Chi from the pages of a book. Traditionally the practice was handed down from master to pupil. Today most large towns offer Tai Chi classes, and anyone wishing to learn its ways and mysteries should join a group.

The classes always begin with a period of meditative stillness, and then the pupils step forward on the right foot—an energy step, with fire being visualized shooting from the palms of the hands. Then the energy is pulled back into the body and the weight transferred to the left foot, everyone now visualizing water cascading over him or her. With the body turning to the left, the palms are rotated and curved back to the right. The body continues to turn to the right with both feet firmly fixed to the floor, then the left foot is brought round, returning the body to the centre.

Tai Chi is a process of self-discovery and, like yoga (*see* page 58), demonstrates the link between body, movement and posture, and contemplative states of being. In the words of one expert, Al Huang, who wrote the classic *Embrace Tiger, Return to Mountain,* 'Tai Chi is to help you get acquainted with your own sense of personal growth, the creative process of just being you.'

Attention to life meditation

This is not meditation in the strictest sense of the word, and it is not a method to be used in daily or twice-daily sessions. Rather, it is part of everyday activity, its object being to focus consciously all your attention on the particular movement, activity or task you are performing to the exclusion of everything else.

Take something as mundane as dishwashing. As you wash each dish, close your eyes and concentrate on feeling each sensation—the warmth of the water, the texture of the plate, the soapiness of the lather, the smell of the detergent. Focus on each part of the activity. To do so, consciously relax all the muscles not essential to the task and work the muscles actually being used as sparingly as possible.

In focusing your thinking on the task in hand in as concentrated a manner as possible, you are actually meditating, albeit for a very short time, but it is surprising how effective such short-span meditation can be, especially in helping to remove feelings of stress.

Meditation on the run

Many long-distance runners hit a point, usually about three-quarters of an hour into a run, when they experience what is commonly called a 'high'. This is remarkably similar to what happens during mantra or chanting meditation, with the rhythmic repetition of the word or phrase being replaced by the

34

rhythm of the run. The runner's conscious mind shuts down, allowing other areas of consciousness to open up.

So, if you enjoy a jog, use it not just to make the body fit, but to put your mind in better shape too.

Don't try to compete with other runners in the park or against the clock to beat your own personal best time. If you do, you are shutting your mind to the possibility of meditation.

Run easily, establishing a regular rhythm, and focus your attention on your breathing, your pulse and heartbeat, and after a while you will reach a point where you will be as perfectly in tune with the world as a Buddhist monk sitting hour after hour in contemplative meditation.

7

Mantra

Repeating a word or phrase—a mantra—over and over again is probably the most practised and widespread path to meditation and one of the oldest. Mantra yoga is mentioned in the *Vedas*, the oldest of the world's scriptures. The mantra may be chanted aloud or repeated silently. The repetition of the mantra is known in India as *japa*, and according to the traditions of that country there are fourteen different kinds of *japa*. Today, in the West, only two of them are in common use—voiced repetition and mental repetition.

The power of the mantra is the power of sound to affect people and alter their state of mind. If you doubt that sound can do this, pause for a moment and consider how irritated you get if someone is playing music too loudly or if you are sitting next to someone who is plugged into a personal stereo and the music is almost audible to you. If sound can irritate, then surely the converse is true—sound can make you feel tranquil, and to focus on a mantra during meditation can lead to some of the deepest and most profound sessions you are likely to experience.

Sound is energy produced by a vibrating object. It is transmitted by waves of different frequencies. Followers of mantra meditation believe that different sounds resonate with different energy centres in the body and that these sounds can be combined in the form of the mantra.

Most of the major religions have their own mantra, and a selection of these are at the end of this section. For those who wish to use a mantra in their meditation but who want to avoid religion, any word or phrase, no matter how meaningless, will do.

In India, until the eleventh century, it was usual for gurus to devise personal mantras for each of their pupils. Each pupil treasured his mantra and refused to divulge it to his fellows for he had been warned that in doing so the power of the mantra would be weakened. In the eleventh century, Ramanuja, a leading figure in the history of Indian yoga and one suspicious of the almost mystical power of the gurus, shouted his mantra from the roof of a temple so that all could share it. The practice of secret mantras now only survives, generally speaking, in the school of Transcendental Meditation (TM) practised by the Maharishi Mahesh.

Those who are suspicious of any religious aspects associated with mantra can do little better than choose their mantra by the method recommended by a Lawrence LeShant, a leading expert in the subject. He advocates the 'La-de' method of mantra selection: simply opening a telephone directory at random and blindly letting the forefinger fall on the page. The first syllable of that name becomes the first syllable of the mantra. Repeat the process, linking the second syllable selected at random with the first and—hey presto!—you have a mantra.

To practise meditation with a mantra, begin, as usual, by taking up the position that you find most comfortable and breathe gently and rhythmically through the nostrils, taking the breath deep into the abdomen. Then repeat the mantra, either aloud or silently inward, focusing your concentration on it as completely as you can. When your mind has become still, it is no longer necessary to continue repeating the mantra, but, as with other forms of meditation, when you become aware that your thoughts have wandered, start repeating the mantra again, concentrating your conscious thoughts on it.

Once you have chosen a mantra with which you are comfortable, stick with it. It's amazing how in times of stress, repeating your mantra a few times silently to yourself restores calm and helps you to put things into proper perspective.

Many mantra meditators repeat the mantra in rhythm with their breathing, saying it once or twice on inhalation and once or twice on breathing out. They are usually repeated silently, but some teachers encourage their pupils to say them aloud, especially if they are leading a group meditation.

Om

Om, a Sanskrit word pronounced to rhyme with 'Rome' is one of the most widely used mantras. According to Hindu belief, *om* is the primal sound and it is accorded the highest value as an object of meditation and one well worth trying. Breathe in gently, and as you exhale recite the word as three sounds, 'a' (as in father), 'oo' (as in room) and 'mmm'. Try to feel the sounds vibrating in your body. The 'a' will feel as if it is ringing in your belly, the 'oo' will resonate in your chest and the 'mmm' will positively resound in the bones of your skull. Link the sounds to your breathing rhythm, keeping it slow and calm and avoiding deepening it in any way.

After saying *om* aloud for ten breaths, soften the voice until you are saying the word under your breath, then lower it even further, keeping your attention firmly focused on it. It won't be long before your lips stop moving and the syllables lose their shape, leaving you with just an idea that clings to your mind. Banish any intrusive thoughts by imagining them as puffs of smoke and watch them being blown away by a gentle breeze.

The Jesus prayer

Some Christians use the name of Jesus as their mantra, others use short prayers, one of the most popular of which is the Jesus prayer which was probably devised by Orthodox monks. It has two forms, either 'Lord Jesus Christ, son of God, have mercy on me', or 'Lord Jesus Christ, have mercy on me'. The prayer follows the advice of a seventh-century mystic who is reputed to have written, 'If many words are used in prayer, all sorts of distracting pictures hover in the mind, but worship is lost. If little is said . . . the mind remains concentrated.' His words could be paraphrased to define mantra—a few words to concentrate the mind.

The rosary

You do not have to be Roman Catholic to meditate on the rosary; any Christian can use the beads as a focus for their meditation. With your eyes closed, pass the beads slowly through the fingers, noticing how the smaller beads are periodically punctuated by large ones. Each time you finger a small bead repeat the words of the Hail Mary:

> Hail Mary, full of grace,
> The Lord is with thee.
> Blessed art thou among women
> And blessed is the fruit of thy womb, Jesus.
> Hail Mary, Mother of God,
> Pray for us sinners now
> And at the hour of our death.
> Amen

Move on to the next bead: if it is small, repeat the Hail Mary, if it is one of the larger beads, say the Lord's Prayer. The meditation should last for the usual twenty minutes.

Humming like a bee

While not a mantra in the true sense of the word, there are many people who hum while meditating. If you would like to try this, take up your usual position but close your right nostril with your right thumb and inhale through the left nostril, holding your breath as deep and as low in the abdomen as you can. Now exhale and as you do so make a humming noise deep in your throat, focusing your thoughts on the sound.

Do this five times and repeat the exercise with the right nostril, then alternate five times with each nostril for the full twenty-minute meditation.

Transcendental Meditation

This form of mantra meditation was introduced to the West in 1959 by the Maharishi Mahesh and became popular in the 1960s when several influential young men and women, pop stars prominent amongst them, claiming they were disillusioned with Western values, turned to the East for spiritual fulfilment. Its central feature is contemplation on and repetition of a Sanskrit mantra personally bestowed on each follower by his or her guru, originally Mahesh himself.

In the Maharishi's own words, in TM '. . . the attention comes from outside to the inside, to the source of thought, and then the conscious mind . . . gains that transcendent pure awareness which is bliss consciousness. It is just thinking, but thinking in a manner so that awareness goes deep within and gains that inner being of pure consciousness.'

Those who follow TM meditate for forty minutes a day in two periods of twenty minutes, repeating their mantra inwardly without moving the lips. The two periods of meditation must be separated by at least six hours of normal activity. Unlike many other Indian schools of meditation, TM demands no conscious changes in lifestyle. The Maharishi claims that such changes will happen spontaneously as the meditation sessions progress.

A great deal of research was conducted on TM, and it emerged that it did create significant psychological changes associated with relaxation. Sceptics, however, queried the methodology of much of the research, and their constant barracking weakened the validity of some of the findings. Those who follow TM insist on the mantra being chosen with much ceremony and in secrecy by the master teacher, but this practice has not been shown to be any more effective than one that uses simple words.

Who says what:

Faith	Mantra	Meaning
Buddhism	Gate, Gate, Pargate, Paramsagate, Bodhi Svahag	Gone, gone, gone to the other shore, safely passed to that other shore, Enlightened One

Namo Buddya, Namo Dharmaya, Namo Sangbaya	I go to the Buddha for refuge, I go to the Dharma for refuge, I go to the Sangha for refuge
Bhagavan Sarva Tathagatha Tathagatha	Blessed be all your Buddhas
Om Tare Tutare Ture Swaha	Hail to Tara
Namo Amitabha	I go to the Buddha for light
Om Mani Padme Hum	Hail to the Jewel in the Lotus

Buddhist mantras are associated with mandalas—images of the cosmos, prayer wheels and beads and counters. It is common among Buddhists to repeat the mantra 108 times because of the numbers: 1 = the absolute; 0 is the cosmos; and 8 is the infinite.

Sikh	*Eck Ong Kar Sat Nam Siri Wha Guru*	The Supreme is one, His names are many
Hindu	*Tat Tuam Asi*	Thou art that
	So ham	That I am
	Hare Krishna	Hail to Krishna
	Hare Rama	Hail to Rama
	Om Namah Sivaya, Shanti, Shanti	Om reverence to Shiva, peace peace

The following mantras have particular healing associations for Hindus:

Hrim (throat and liver)

Hrum (liver and spleen)

Hraim (kidneys)

Hra (heart and chest)

41

Islam	*Allah, Allah,*	God, God, there is no God but
	La Ilaha Illa'llah	one God
	Insha Allah	If God wills
	Ya-Salaam	God, the source of peace
	An-Nur	God, the light
Judaism	*Adonai*	Lord
	Shalom	Peace
	Ehyeh Asher Ehyeh	I am that I am
	Quadosh, Quadosh,	Holy, Holy, Holy Lord of Hosts
	Quadosh Adonai	
	Tzeba'oth	
	Eli, Eli, Eli	My God, My God, My God
	Barukh Ata Adonai	Blessed is the Lord
Christian	*Lord Jesus Christ,*	
	Son of God, Have	
	Mercy on us	
	Kyrie Eleison, Christe	Lord have mercy, Christ have
	Eleison, Kyrie Eleison	mercy, God have mercy
	Laudamus	We praise thee
	Alleluia	
	Holy, Holy, Holy	
	En Emoi Christus	Christ in me
	Ave Maria	Hail Mary
Sufism	*Hu-E-Haiy*	God the living
	He-La	The word is the mirror wherein the Divine reverberates outwardly. Through sound the world will be reabsorbed. The word is both sound and light, for light is the meaning of the word

8

Visual Meditation

Visual meditation uses our natural capacity to think in pictures and our ability to create images in what is often called the mind's eye. It may be practised with the eyes open or shut or by opening and shutting them for alternate periods, concentrating on the after-image that remains in our mind when the eyes are closed. The latter method is most usually recommended for beginners.

Place the object of your meditation (on which more later) at eye level between a metre and two metres from your face. If you decide to use a mandala or yantra (*see* page 46) the central point should be level with the eyes. Assume whichever meditation position you favour, and in as relaxed a way as possible, gaze at the image, focusing your attention on it, trying to become *absorbed* in what you are looking at rather than just thinking about it. After two or three minutes or as soon as you feel any sign of eye strain, close your eyes and visualize the object for as long as you can, still trying to be part of it. Open the eyes again and continue alternating open-eyed and closed-eyed meditation for the full session.

Initially it will be difficult to retain the image in your mind's eye for long when your eyes are closed: don't worry. When the image starts to fade, open the eyes and gaze at the object again. As you become more practised in the art, you will find that you can retain the image for longer and longer.

Meditating on a candle
Many of those who come to visual meditation for the first time find that a lighted candle in a darkened room is the ideal object of focus. One method recommended for beginners is to light a candle in a darkened, draught-free room, draught-free so that

the flame burns as steadily as possible. To meditate on a candle, sit as motionless as you can in any of the recommended positions and gaze at the flame so that it holds your attention completely. Let the image fill your mind for a minute before quickly closing the eyes. Notice how the candle has imprinted itself on the darkness. Hold it in your mind's eye, not worrying about any change of colour. If it slips to the side, bring it back to the centre and keep concentrating until the image fades completely. Now open the eyes and resume gazing at the candle. Continue in this way for ten minutes at first, gradually increasing the time until you can sit comfortably for a full twenty-minutes.

A flower or a bowl
Some people begin their visualizing techniques with a flower. One expert tells his novice pupils to gaze at a patterned china bowl, taking it all in at first, then allowing the eyes to travel over it, tracing its lines and colours, the pattern that decorates it, the way it catches the light. Only when his pupils come to experience the bowl's visual qualities for the first time, does he move on to telling them to close their eyes and try to focus on the image of the bowl held in the mind.

It takes practice
At first, it is hard to hold a mental picture of the object, but with practice it becomes easier and easier until the point is reached when the actual object can be abandoned completely and you can meditate on the mental image with no external visual stimulus being used. This can be extremely difficult, and if you have been successful with the alternating method but have had problems when you have tried to meditate holding a mental image in your mind for the entire session, you have probably been trying too hard or expecting too much. It can take years of practice before you can see the image clearly. Think of the mind as a musical instrument that has to be tuned

with patience and sensitivity before it can be used to produce beautiful music.

Some who practise visual meditation find it helps to train the mind by closing the eyes and picturing a friend, concentrating on each feature in turn, the colour of the skin and hair, the shape and colour of the eyes, and so on, and then returning to the complete face, holding on to the image for as long as they can, and when it starts to blur, focusing again on the separate features.

Many different symbols

Roman Catholics and Anglicans have long used the image of Christ on the cross as a symbol in visualization meditation. Christians who belong to the 'low' Churches often meditate on the empty cross, while many people who belong to the Orthodox Church use small painted panels bearing an image of Christ or the Virgin Mary or any of the saints as visualization symbols.

Buddhists may meditate on a mental image of Buddha himself or one of the other Buddhas, especially Tara, the liberator, the mother of all Buddhas. They see her as the manifestation of all that is positive. Bathed in radiant emerald-green light, swathed in silk and bedecked with jewels, she smiles lovingly at those who focus their meditations on her.

Jewish meditators might visualize the Tree of Life that represents the *Sefirot,* or ten divine energies.

The *Visuddhimagga,* a fourth-century Buddhist text, lists ten different subjects for visual meditation. These are known as *kasinas* and comprise air, earth, fire and water (the four elements), blue, yellow, red and green (the four colours of nature), light and space. To meditate on any of the elements, the meditator simply stares at an appropriate object, a pot filled with earth, for example, or a bowl of water. To visualize any of the four colours, simply gaze at an object of that colour—a flower, a piece of fabric, anything at all. To meditate on light, focus the attention on the light cast by a lightbulb, and any empty container can be used as a focus when meditating on space.

Buddhists, in common with Hindus, also use *mandalas*, the most famous of which is probably the Buddhist wheel of life, and Hindus commonly meditate on *yantras* (*see* below).

Chinese meditators often use the famous Yin-yang symbol. It looks like a white tadpole with a black eye and a black tadpole with a white eye, curled up against each other, their outline forming a perfect circle representing tai chi (supreme ultimate).

Yantras and mandalas

To scholars of Sanskrit, *yantra* is a word meaning 'instrument', and *mandala* is a word that means 'circle'—the supreme universal symbol. To the meditator, a yantra is a diagram that possesses the power to transform the consciousness of those who have been introduced to knowledge of what the yantras represent.

A mandala is essentially a type of yantra, the yantra being more specific to a particular deity, the mandala being more general. Both are diagrammatic in form, designed so that the focus of the meditator comes to rest on a central focal point, the *bindu,* which is said to represent the essence of being.

They can be astonishingly beautiful to look at, especially those of Tibetan Tantric Buddhists whose richly symbolic and gloriously designed mandalas have come to be prized by collectors as works of art.

(There is another aspect of Tantric Buddhism that westerners find fascinating, mistaking it more often than not as an indulgence of the sexual appetites rather than a tool for meditation—*maithuna*, or ritual sexual intercourse. Those who practise it claim that it is a potent means of allowing *kundalini* energy—the force awakened by meditation on the chakras (*see* below)—to be released, allowing the yogi to move on to meditating a higher chakra. Before performing maithuna, the yogi performs certain rituals and recites the mantra given to

46

him by his guru as well as other mantras that are part of the rituals. Maithuna must be carried out in the prescribed manner, the yogi having been taught exactly where and how he may touch his partner's body. It is the female who is active during maithuna, since its aim is the arousal of energy rather than the climax, at which moment the yogi consecrates his semen as a sacrificial offering.)

The lotus blossom, the symbol of enlightenment, is widely used as part of the patterns, symbolizing the unfolding of creation. According to Hindu mythology, Brahma stood at the centre of a thousand-petalled lotus before creating the universe, and Buddhists believe that at the birth of the Buddha, a large lotus sprang from the earth, and Buddha stepped into its centre. From there he gazed into the ten directions of space, once along each of the eight petals, once upwards and once downwards.

Mandalas and yantras may be drawn, painted or carved in stone. Some eastern mystics even meditate on yantras that they draw for themselves in the sand or earth. Such temporary ones often serve as teaching aids between master and pupils.

Meditating with a mandala or yantra

Before you can meditate with a mandala or yantra you will have to be instructed on its meaning. Then, place it so that the central point is at eye level when you are sitting before it in your usual meditating position. Relax the muscles of your face and sit absolutely motionless, gazing at the centre point. Let your gaze move slowly outwards to the edge, taking in but trying not to think about the visual content. Now let the gaze move slowly back to the centre before closing the eyes and holding the image in your mind's eye for as long as you can before opening the eyes again and repeating the process. As you become more practised, you will find that your eye will automatically be drawn to the centre and that it rests there effortlessly on the point that symbolizes the essence of being.

Chakras

Some schools of yoga (*see* page 58), believe that there are centres of psychic energy, or *chakras,* placed in the *sushumna,* the central canal of the astral body roughly corresponding to the spinal column in the physical body. The chakras sit at various points between the base of the spine and the top of the head. Two schools of yoga, Tantric and Kundalini, practise meditation on each of them in turn.

Each chakra has its own yantra and its own mantra (apart from the topmost one). Starting with the lowest of them, the *muladhara,* situated between the anus and genitals, the meditator visualizes its yantra while repeating its mantra, either inwardly or aloud, until ready to move on.

As the meditation works its way through the chakra, the latent energy of each one is released, imbuing the meditator with stronger and stronger sensations of warmth and light at the centre until, when the final meditation is completed, the physical will have merged with the spiritual—the meditator's consciousness merges with the universe.

Each chakra is adorned with its own number of lotus petals, governed by the number of the body channels that conjoin at that point in the astral body. The muladhara is adorned with four such petals and its mantra is '*lam*'. In ascending order the chakras are the six-petalled *svadhishtana*: its mantra is '*vam*'. The *manipura* has ten petals and its mantra is '*ram*'. Next comes the *anahata,*with twelve petals and the mantra '*yam*'. Then, with sixteen petals and the mantra '*ham*', is the *vishuddha* chakra. The *ajna* chakra, with its two petals and the mantra '*om*' is next, followed by the topmost, the *sahasrara,* or thousand-petal chakra, which has no mantra.

Anyone wishing to practise this form of meditation needs detailed instruction from an experienced teacher over a long period of time, but the following meditation may give you just a flavour of the full effect.

The space between the eyebrows meditation

This space corresponds to the ajna chakra. Sit, kneel or lie in your usual position with your eyes closed. Gently swivel your eyeballs upwards and try to visualize them as focused on the space between your eyebrows. See how close this space is to the brain—feel its central position, visualize viewing it from the outside: now visualize it from the inside. The space between the eyebrows is a part of you. As the meditation deepens feel yourself becoming a part of that space. If unwanted thoughts intrude, mentally blow them away and return your focus to the space between the eyebrows.

It is not possible here to describe the whys and wherefores of every type of visual meditation. But the ones described below have all been used successfully by meditators the world over.

Colour visualizing

There are many methods of using colour as a means of reaching the meditative state. The two given here are among the simplest.

For the first, sit in whichever position you favour and begin to breathe deeply. As usual, don't force the breath, but let it find its own pace and depth. When it has settled to a slow, rhythmic rate, begin to visualize the colours red, orange and yellow, flowing upwards into your solar plexus, visualizing each colour one at a time as a gently flowing river.

Spend a minute or so on each colour and then picture a stream of green flowing into the solar plexus from directly in front of you. After a minute or so, follow the green with blue, indigo and violet, each in turn flowing into you from the same source as the green.

Once the spectrum is completed, imagine yourself bathed in a blue light before ending the meditation by opening your eyes.

Don't be put off if at first you find it difficult to visualize a colour: with practice this becomes easier.

The second method is to sit with eyes closed before focusing the thoughts on any colour you wish. Fill your mind with that colour to the exclusion of everything else and refuse to be frustrated by other thoughts that may come to mind. Wrap them slowly in the colour so that they are enveloped in it. It sometimes helps to imagine an object of your chosen shade—a field of yellow corn perhaps—and gradually concentrate your thoughts on it until the field becomes totally unimportant and your mind is a canvas of yellow. (Some people who practise colour meditation, in fact, begin each session by picturing an easel on which rests a blank canvas that stroke by stroke fills up with the chosen colour.)

Body of light visualizing

This is an advanced meditation. Sit comfortably with your back straight, breathing naturally. When your mind is clear and calm, visualize the space above your head as a sphere of white light slightly smaller in size than your head. Try to see it as pure and transparent, and spend several minutes concentrating on it.

See the sphere of light as representing goodness, wisdom and love—as the fulfilment of your own highest potential. Then visualize that it is getting smaller and smaller until it is about two centimetres in diameter and that slowly it begins to descend through your head towards your heart, then begins to expand once more until it spreads to every part of your body. As it does so, see it dissolve all the organs and solid parts of your body until they too become pure, formless white light.

Concentrate on the perception of your body as a mass of light and believe all your problems, negative emotions and the things that hold you back have vanished. Let any thoughts or distractions dissolve in the light, and with practice you will achieve a joyful serenity and reach a state of wholeness and perfection.

Purification visualizing

Purification is a recurring theme in Buddhist meditation. When we see ourselves as impure or negative, that is what we become. With our self-esteem at a low ebb we feel limited and inadequate and don't give ourselves a chance to change. Believing we are pure in essence is the first step to becoming pure in practice.

This simple meditation contains the essence of purification, banishing problems and mistakes, trying to see them as temporary instructions, not as part of our nature.

Begin by settling comfortably into a suitable position, then concentrate on breathing normally and observing how long each exhalation and inhalation lasts. After a minute or two, imagine that all your negative energy, the mistakes you have made in the past, the things that are holding you back are leaving your body in a cloud of black smoke each time you breathe out. When you inhale, visualize that everything positive in the universe is entering your body in a stream of white light, as radiant as it is pure. Visualize it flowing to every part of your body, bathing it in its intensity.

Banish distractions by seeing them as black smoke and exhale them along with the other negative aspects of your experience.

Bubbles of thought meditation

Sitting in a comfortable position, visualize your mind as the smooth, calm surface of a pond. As thoughts enter your mind, see them as bubbles rising from the depths of the pond. They should be observed, not pursued, so that the conscious and deliberate following through of each thought is avoided and you become detached from it as you watch it bubble to the surface. Note the thought and then gently return to contemplating the smooth, rippleless surface of the pond.

As time passes and you pass into deeper layers of consciousness, see yourself sinking under the surface of the pond, becoming one with it.

After about ten minutes, refocus your mind on your surroundings to bring the meditation to an end.

Inner heat meditation

This is an extremely advanced meditation requiring sophisticated breathing techniques as well as visualization. It is included here as an example of the most demanding meditation techniques. It was developed by a Tibetan Buddhist who believed that mental energy flows through the body within an invisible psychic nervous system made up of thousands of thin, transparent channels. The principal ones—the central, right and left channels—run parallel to and just in front of the spinal column. Pure mental energy can function within the central channel whereas diluted (deluded) energy flows through the others.

In our normal state, the central channel is blocked by knots of nervous energy at the various chakras discussed above (*see* page 48). This energy blocks pure energy from the mind, making it unable to function properly.

Inner heat meditation is an excellent method for transforming powerful negative energy, helping us to develop spontaneous control over all actions of body, speech and mind.

Begin by adopting your usual meditation posture, settle your thoughts and your breathing, and visualize the central channel as a transparent, hollow tube, about the same diameter as your forefinger, running straight down the centre of the body just in front of the spinal column, from the crown of your head to the base of your spine.

Now visualize the left and right channels, slightly thinner than the central one, starting from the left and right nostril respectively, reaching up to the top of the head then curving to run downwards on either side of the central channel before curving inwards to join the central channel about a hand's-breadth below the navel.

Take your time. There is no hurry whatsoever, and once the visualization (some people say it helps to see it as a very simple central heating system) is firmly fixed, imagine a red-hot ember the size of a seed inside the central channel level with the navel. If it helps to strengthen this visualization, see yourself reaching into a fire and taking out a small ember that you put in place.

When you really feel the intense heat, gently contract the lower pelvic muscles and see air energy rising from the lowest chakra up to the ember. Now breathe deeply through both nostrils, seeing the air travelling down the left and right channels round into the central channel, where it joins with the heat and air energy brought up from below.

When you have inhaled, swallow and push down gently with the diaphragm, compressing the energy brought down from above: the air energy is locked in, trapped from above and below.

Now hold the breath as long as possible without forcing it and concentrate on the glowing ember in the navel area, its heat now spreading through the compressed air energy.

When you breathe out, visualize the warm air rising through the central channel, seeing it burn away the negative energies blocking each of the chakras.

Repeat the cycle seven times, intensifying the heat with each breath. By the time you breathe out for the seventh time, visualize the ember bursting into flames, shooting up the central channel and burning out the remaining negative energy in the chakras. When the flames reach the crown of the head, they melt into wonderful, almost sensual, energy that rushes down the now pure central channel, intensifying in pleasure as it passes each chakra, finally engulfing the remains of the ember and making it explode in a blissful heat that reaches every cell of your body, filling you with happiness.

If you ever succeed in this meditation, don't try to analyse the bliss, just accept it, relax, enjoy and concentrate on it calmly and in a controlled manner. It is, as we said, extremely complex, but those who have mastered it believe it is, the best of all visual meditation techniques.

Visual meditation and health

Although the following is not meditation in the true sense of the word, visualization is required, and we demonstrate how it can be used to treat two specific health problems. Space precludes us from dealing with more ailments and how they may be treated, but if you try the ones discussed below, perhaps you may be tempted to look further into this area: it can be extremely rewarding.

Assume your usual meditation posture unless your malady prevents it, in which case, make yourself as comfortable as you can with the back as straight as you can get it and the head in perfect alignment. Concentrate on your breathing for a moment or two until it becomes settled and regular.

For *painful joints,* picture the affected area in your mind and visualize the blood vessels leading to and from it congested with dark red blood. Notice how taut the muscles are and how tangled the nerves. With this image firmly fixed, see a tide of pink, oxygen-full blood enriched with healing white cells flood through the veins and arteries. Observe how the muscles relax and your nerves untangle. Hold this image in your mind and then visualize the whole area again free from congestion, the muscles working smoothly, the nerves strands of polished wire. Let the image fade from view and, hopefully, the pain will have eased.

For *bronchial problems,* visualize your lungs clogged with dark yellow mucus. Now see the colour lighten, starting from the bottom of each lung until the mucous membranes are producing just enough mucus to keep the lungs properly lubricated and there is a ball of mucus being pushed up your throat and coughed out. You should be breathing much more easily at the end of this visualization.

Similar techniques, where the affected area is visualized first in its stricken state then as being cleansed before being seen in perfect working order, can be applied to a whole host of complaints. When all else fails, why not try them?

9

Other Techniques To Try

Tactile meditation

Before you begin, choose an object to hold while you are
meditating—something light, for if it is too heavy its weight will
affect your concentration and hence your focus. It need not be
soft, but it should not be sharp. Now close your eyes and
concentrate on the texture of the object in your hand, focusing
on how it feels rather than what it is.

Another method of using touch to help reach the meditative
state requires either a set of worry beads or four or five
pebbles. Relax in your favourite position, holding the beads or
pebbles in the open palm of one hand and with the other move
them rhythmically and methodically between your fingers,
counting them one at a time.

Feel each bead or pebble as you count, focusing all your
attention on the slow, repetitive movement.

Music and meditation

The relevance of music as an aid to meditation is a personal
one. Its effect depends on facilitating your meditations, and that
in turn depends on your own instincts and intuitions.

Percussion instruments have long been used in meditation,
especially where it is practised by atavists. The music they
produce symbolizes rhythm and vitality.

Gongs and bells are said to purify the surrounding atmosphere
making it more conducive to meditation. Many religions use peals
of bells to help their adherents regather wandering thoughts. If
you want to use bells as an aid to meditation, focus your thoughts
on the sound, trying to experience it beyond audibility.

Harps have long been associated with meditation. In China the *cheng* and other zither-like instruments are widely used, while in India, the sitar and the vina accompany meditative chanting.

The gentle tinkling of the Aeolian harp can create a perfectly calm state of mind as you approach your meditations, and help you to focus your thought.

To meditate to music, take up your usual position, close your eyes and listen to a favourite piece, immersing yourself in it completely. Try to become one with the sound, letting the sound encompass you, and if your thoughts are invaded by memories associated with the piece you have selected, imagine them as musical notes floating off into the distance.

Zen meditation
The word 'Zen' derives from the Sanskrit *dhyana,* meaning 'meditation'. With its roots in the Yisuddhimagga tradition, it is widely practised in Japan, having arrived there through the Ch'an meditation school of China.

Zen's main practice is *zazen,* or sitting on a cushion facing a wall, and is done daily by those who practise it, usually adopting the full lotus position. Meditation sessions are quite lengthy, hence, in zazen, great stress is placed on correct posture. The body is held upright, and it should be theoretically possible to draw a line from the centre of the forehead down through the nose, chin, throat, navel into the coccyx at the tail of the spine. Every part of the body must be in balance: if it is not, incorrect balance in one part of the body will cause strain in another and ruin the meditation.

The left hand rests within the right, the middle joints of the middle fingers touching, with the thumbs, also lightly touching each other, held at the navel and the arms slightly away from the rest of the body.

Apart from the fact that novices to Zen are sometimes advised to count their breaths, from one to ten, and the use of *koan* (*see* below), zazen uses no mantra, mandala or other object of meditation. In zazen, thoughts are allowed to come

56

and go without being banished by the meditator, who remains attentive and alert throughout the meditation, concentrating on sitting as still as possible in a state of quiet awareness.

Zen masters often ask their pupils impenetrable questions, known as koan, an unanswerable puzzle designed to precipitate awakening by breaking through the limited confines of consciousness. A common one is 'What was your face before you were born?' From then on, whenever the koan comes to mind, the pupil banishes all other thoughts and concentrates on his koan. As he comes to realize that there is no answer *per se*, he reaches a state that has been described by those who have achieved it as 'feverish concentration', from which arises 'supreme frustration', and with conscious thought transcended, the pupil attains *samadhi,* the state of total concentration.

The first koan is said to have arisen when the great Zen master Hui-neng was attacked by robbers. He begged them to be silent for a moment and then said to them, 'When you are thinking of neither good nor evil, what is at that moment your original face?' The assailants were so astonished that they begged Hui for an explanation. The master sent them on their way, and the men found that the question came to dominate their thoughts to such an extent that when something else came to mind, they banished it and resumed their meditation on the question until they found they had arrived at samadhi.

10

Yoga

It is not possible in this brief introduction to meditation to go too deeply into yoga. Every library in the land contains shelf after shelf of books on the history and practice of the subject, and a community centre notice board will usually display a card advertising a local yoga class.

If, after reading this brief outline of the subject, you decide to try yoga as a means to meditation, you would be well advised to join such a class, for to get the best out of yoga, a good teacher is required. Avoid a multidiscipline teacher (and this also applies when looking for a teacher to guide you in any form of meditation). Someone who claims to be able to teach yoga, Tai Chi *and* Sufi dancing will usually turn out to be a jack of all trades and master of none

Back to yoga!

Yoga is a technique of self-awareness that integrates the mind and the body. The word derives from the Sanskrit *yuj* meaning 'to bind together', and through practising yoga, the yogi tries to bind himself with the universal process of being.

Yoga recognizes the interrelatedness of mind and body. Hatha yoga teaches techniques of physical control of the body through postures known as *asanas* and breathing techniques called *pranayama*. The asanas make the body supple and benefit the neuromuscular system, each posture combining mental acuity with breathing techniques and a specific body movement. Pranayama builds up the body's energy.

Yoga is a means of seeing things as they really are rather than as they seem. In Yoga, all body and mental tensions have to cease if this end is to be achieved. Accordingly, one of the basic yoga techniques is meditation, which turns our consciousness towards the inner calm helping us to achieve *samadhi,* or pure consciousness.

Sukhasana is one of the basic meditative poses in yoga. In it, the spine is held straight, the legs are crossed, the eyes closed and the head poised above the shoulders. Breathing deeply through the nose, the meditator focuses attention on the rhythm of the breath and concentrates on being.

For yoga to calm the mind, a number of tensions (*klesas*) have to be overcome. These include ignorance, the sense of ego and identification with the body, attention to pleasure, repulsion of pain and the desire for life.

In meditation the yogi becomes united with the object of meditation and the klesas evaporate. To help you achieve this, you may fix the concentration on yantras *(see* page 46) or chakras *(see* page 48).

Yoga lays great emphasis on leading a healthy lifestyle— getting enough sleep, eating plenty of raw fruit and vegetables, cutting down on red meat, alcohol and cigarettes (sensible advice for everyone, not just those who decide to take up yoga), for yogis believe that only when the body is healthy is it an adaptable and obedient instrument for manifesting the self.

The yoga salute
A yoga class that lasts for one or two hours and ends with deep relaxation is classic meditation in itself. It is possible to experience the same effect on your own by doing the yoga salute to the sun for twenty minutes or so.

It coordinates breathing with variations of six yoga poses that stretch your body in a flowing rhythmic way and relax your body and your mind to create a subtle shift into meditation.

Start by facing east, standing up as straight as you can, without forcing it, with your feet together. Inhale and visualize the sun just beginning to rise. Exhale and bring the palms of the hands on to your chest as if you were praying.

Inhale again, stretching your arms overhead as you do so, pushing the pelvis forward a little, and look up at your hands.

Breathe out, bending slowly from your waist until, ideally, your hands are touching the floor in front of or beside your feet. (Don't force this: if you can't reach the floor, let your hands hold on to the lowest part of your legs they can reach.)

Breathe in and lunge forward by bending your left knee to a right angle and stepping your right foot back. Turn your toes right under and straighten your body from head to heel. Holding your breath, move the left foot back, toes curled until you are in the classic push-up position. Now exhale and drop your knees to the floor, with your bottom up. Bend the elbows and bring your chest and chin to the floor. Continue breathing out and lower the whole body to the floor, straightening your legs and keeping your toes curled under.

Inhale, pushing down on your hands and slowly lifting your head as you straighten the elbows. Arch your back upwards like a snake before it strikes.

Breathe out and, with the buttocks as high as you can raise them and the head down, form a pyramid.

Breathe in and lunge forward by bending your right knee and stepping your right foot forward between your hands. When you breathe out, straighten your right leg and bring the left foot next to the right. Lift your buttocks high until you are touching your toes.

Inhale and slowly lift the spine, visualizing it unroll one vertebra at a time. Raise your head and look up, bringing your arms straight overhead, and bring the image of the rising sun back to mind.

Breathe out and slowly bring your arms back to the sides, allowing the sun to glow brighter and brighter in your mind's eye.

Salute the sun six times at first, gradually increasing the

number of repetitions until you are comfortably doing the routine 24 times. As you come to perfect it without consciously thinking of each body movement, once your rhythm becomes smoother and you coordinate each step with your breathing, then you will find that you will have been meditating as efficiently as if you had been sitting in deep contemplation for hour after hour after hour.

The dharanas

Yoga is perhaps the only discipline that encourages meditation on sex. Such meditation is found in the *Vijnanabhairava,* an ancient book on yoga that is essentially a dialogue between Shiva and his enlightened consort. When she asks Shiva how the supreme state can be realized, Shiva suggests 112 *dharanas* or centring techniques, that enable those who practise them to attain divine consciousness. Among the dharanas is one that suggests meditating on the delights of a remembered intensely pleasurable sexual experience. In practice, the meditator must turn his or her attention away from the actual experience and trace the pleasure back to its source—the inner self.

The *Vijnanabhairava* also promotes the Hamsah meditation technique. By it, the meditator watches the breath going in and coming out, making a *ha* sound with each inhalation and a *sah* sound to accompany each exhalation. The *m* is inserted between the two other sounds. Hamsah is often called 'the universal mantra'.

11

Grabbing the Moment Meditation

Once you gain experience in meditating, it is possible to go into meditative mode for short periods whenever you need to. All it takes to meditate in this way is a few seconds of concentrated focus, and you will find yourself refreshed and ready to cope with stress. We have used the right in hand some of the meditations described below: if you are left-handed, use the thumb and two fingers of the left hand instead.

The wedding ring meditation

To meditate on your wedding ring, simply inhale deeply and bring the tip of the thumb on whichever hand you wear your wedding ring into contact with the first two fingers so that the ring finger is slightly raised. As you exhale slowly, focus your eyes on the ring, gazing at a glint that catches the light. Repeat four or five times.

The red light meditation

Next time you are held up at traffic lights, stare at the red light with both eyes, willing yourself into it. Breathe in and out slowly as many times as you can until the lights change, and you will take off in a better frame of mind than before.

Meditation at work

Most people have jobs that involve doing the same thing day after day, be it something as active as waiting tables in a restaurant or as sedentary as working in an office in front of a computer. Most people at some time or other during their working day find themselves drifting off into their own thoughts: use this time to improve your work efficiency by meditating. The moment you first realize you are lost in thought, visualize a blank screen and then picture yourself on that